nappyminded ideology

[**nap**-ee-**mahyn**-did id-ee-**ol**-*uh*-jee]

- the perception of blackness from black eyes.

nappyminded ideology

by
LAQUITA MIDDLETON-HOLMES

NEW GRIOT SOCIETY PRESS
| BIRMINGHAM |

ISBN-13: 978-0615724744 (New Griot Society Press)
ISBN-10: 0615724744

For more info on New Griot Society Press and author, please visit:

www.Visionary-Tours.com
(205) 467-8713

NEW GRIOT SOCIETY PRESS
PO BOX 91
BIRMINGHAM, AL 35201

nappyminded ideology

forward

Having been in the struggle for human dignity since the age of seven at the Historic Bethel Baptist Church in Birmingham, AL, I am honored to share my well wishes for a young lady who is not afraid to let you see, hear, read, and feel her passion for what is right, what is true, and what is fair.

My family survived a devastating bombing on Christmas night in 1956, and with body and faith unscathed, the very next day we rode the buses in efforts to desegregate public transportation. In 1957, Rev. Phieffer drove us away safely from a mob crowd at Phillips High School where Daddy was beaten and Mudear was stabbed for attempting to integrate public schools. We faced many scary situations as Daddy led the Alabama Christian Movement for Human Rights (ACMHR). Thank God for the many brave footsoldiers who guarded our home, marched, encouraged, prayed, and worked nonviolently for human rights. The Magic City was "Bombingham" – a scary place to be at ages 11 and 12. As I read LaQuita's poetry, I feel she is saying what I felt and wanted to say, but didn't know I could.

I met LaQuita at the Birmingham Civil Rights Institute while she was leading a tour. I was amazed at her knowledge and attention to the details of "why" and "how" situations occurred.

She is steeped in African American history and seeks to honor our heritage in all areas of her life. She is never ashamed... of herself or her people, and she always encourages others... teaching history, so that positive knowledge goes forth...

This young lady, Mrs. LaQuita Denise Middleton, calls it like it is! She says,

This is me. This is my life. It has been made better by those who came before me. It is now my duty to provide that opportunity for future generations unapologetically. Civil rights leaders taught that we should not be afraid. They taught that we should love those who espoused hate against us. They taught that we should never be afraid to stand up for freedom and equality. It is upon this revolutionary foundation that I have dedicated my life to teach our history.

I am eternally thankful to her for the care, love, and concern she showed my father while in the nursing homes and hospitals in Birmingham, AL. She was there with her children to make sure he was doing the best that he could. For this I am thankful.

I am honored to write this forward to say to the readers of this book, "Get ready to learn! Get ready to feel! Get ready to lift up your heritage!"

Ruby Shuttlesworth Bester
Daughter of Rev. Fred L. Shuttlesworth

acknowledgments

In all things, I give honor to God who has been my
Jehovah Jireh, Nissi, Rapha, & Shalom.
I love You & will forever bring honor to Your Kingdom.

To my daughters,
Niara Selah aka "Mecca" & Kelsi Yolan aka "Binky."
From helping Mommy memorize poems line by line to
waiting politely until I'm finished reciting a poem to
ask for your sippy cup –
you two are the best D.I.T.'s a Mommy could ask for.
I can't wait to see your names in lights!

To my loving husband, Comedian Terrence G.
Thank you for supporting fully my dreams – however unconventional
they may seem. I'm proud to be "Mrs. G." I love you!

To Sister Gloria Johnson.
Thank you for forcing my "revolutionary" thoughts & beliefs
into poetic form, & for providing me with a waiting stage &
an eager audience.

To Professor Andrew Baskin.
Your classes made me a great writer & thinker.
Thank you for your support & encouragement!

To Mrs. Ruby Shuttlesworth Bester.
Thank you for welcoming me into the family!
It means the world to me that you believe in me & my work.
Your father was the most courageous man I've ever known;
whenever I'm unsure, I am reminded always of his courage.

To the FootSoldiers.
Thank you for braving an America that was steeped in racism &
bigotry for centuries – & treated Black people accordingly.
Your work inspires my words.
I am forever indebted to you.

earrings under the beret

revolution (panther rising)

many people try to stake the claim that
i am nowhere near what is implied by my name—

revolution.

they think that i'm causing pollution in the game, but
i think that they think that i am causing pollution in their
game
because i choose not to spend a lot of time on topics like,

"he loves me, he loves me not"

or recite those abstract poems that leave the audience
wondering,
"what the heck was she talking about?"

yeah, i can do those poems without a sweat, so
don't ever doubt the poetic greatness that the revolution
possesses.

-you see,
i would rather write poems that matter.
be the poet who'll make the people gather.
rally around a cause greater than
writing those same ol' poems about
loving haters and hating love.

you see,
i would rather talk about those things that make <u>me</u> hot

like…

black folks shunning their history
& when they hear it
it's a novel of mystery…
or—

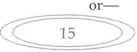

like—

how revolution
has always been the solution
to oppressed people's intrusion
on equal rights.

no freedom has ever come without a price that was too high,
and no wars have ever been won without human casualties.

but yet and still,
we walk around casually
as if the world was created by we,
concerning ourselves with things that will die
with and before you and me.

so, i choose to concern myself with things that will help
change the world.
things that'll make it just a tad bit better for my little girl
whose purpose is greater than mine.

and in due time
she will have her time to shine
leaving her fingerprints behind
for those grandkids of mine.

but until that time,
i'm gon' keep shining
my mirror to the sun
getting the attention of these lost ones....

with the hope that one day, hah!
on the blood streaked streets of birmingham
what i lived my life for
will have freed the shackles from my people's
minds and feet
and that they have the true feeling of being free

in the spirit of lincoln's e. p.
amendment 13
birth of the naacp
brown versus b.o.e.
boycott by rosa louise
cra by kennedy
vra by lyndon
and just a few short months after the election of president
who looks like me...

and when the horns sound when they shout my name:

revolution!!!   revolution!!!   revolution!!!

you best believe i'm coming full-flamed
six-edged sword ready to swang

with no remorse

just staking my claim
that the time for revolution
is now.

and you wonder why i say the revolution be me?

it's because i don't bow down easily
takes more than mace and a strait jacket
to hold me.

you can even taze me.

but i be the revolution
human incarnated.

i be—
no need for conjugation.

but the revelation still remains the same

that i be the revolution
with no convolution.

and if this revolution doesn't start with me,

then how else will we ever get free?

revolution

when will i hear the trumpets sound?

when will Gabriel stand on the edge of Heaven
and blow his horn?

when will africa send out her most talented
musicians, dancers, and drummers
rev up the anger of the people
and cause a real revolution to begin?

in the early '70s,
a revolutionary artist named
gil scott heron
proclaimed that the revolution will not be televised

and i know that in the new millennium
the revolution's gotta at least come with a beat

because that's the only way we can hear it.

and maybe
just maybe
if sean bell would've hummed a nitty beat
as his body hit the cement
maybe it would've sent a
morse code
black hawk down
african tribal call
to people all around
making us actually give a care
about policemen continuing to abuse their power
in this new age and hour.

and maybe
just maybe
if sean bell would've gotten timbaland

to syncopate the beat
and missy elliott to rewind the hook
maybe we would've cared enough to be
shaken, stirred up, and shook up
enough to gather the masses 'round

maybe we would've cared enough to
make sure his killers wouldn't have gone free
leaving the courtroom
silently smiling and high fiving
as his "would've been new wife" steadily crying,

interrogating the gods, "why???"

but maybe
just maybe
it wasn't <u>our</u> fault.

it had to be sean's fault
because he failed to send us that bird call
through that nitty beat.

you see,
he was born guilty.
his melanin level
gave him special treatment
when it comes to meeting and dealing with the police.

in the new millennium
we're still not free.

the land of the free
has never applied to me
or to anybody in my black family.

...if only he would've hummed that nitty beat...
but you see
we've become so desensitized to reality

that we don't realize that the time for nonchalance
has been nullified

the revolution doesn't need to be televised
we just need to open our eyes
and remove ourselves from our tvs,
mp3s, ipods, myspace, clubs, weed and crack shacks,
and realize that the revolution has already started against
us:

the black, the poor, the migrant.

my people, we are too caught up in trivial dreams
that we can't wake up and see
that 40, 50, 60 years ago is repeating itself
right before our weed laden eyes,

and we are soooo hiiiiiigh that
we won't be able to come down fast enough
to do a dang thing about it.

and by the time we realize the revolution is already here,
our evolution will be

gone. nonexistent. finito. over.

when will your trumpeters sound?

america: i am

america: i am
[a woman],   [a man],
[not aunt jemima]   [or uncle ben]

i have earned my keep
my fathers and mothers have all paid the price
sacrificed their lives
and livelihoods
just to live in your neighborhoods,
eat in your restaurants,
and spend their "hard earned, more work for lesser pay"
green dollars in your segregated department stores
because they saw that your separate
wasn't our equal...

white people
your lily white pathologies
have always proven to be hypocrisy
and they no longer work in our eyes
and we don't sympathize...

and, no, we don't apologize
for being born of the darker color
for the original man and woman
was our father and mother

so, no, we won't apologize
bow our heads
and step off your sidewalks
because our mothers are the ones
who taught your children to talk

and once they learned to utter sounds
you turned around and taught them
that we were ordained to kiss their ground.
so, no, i won't apologize

and i don't sympathize

america: i am
the one clothed in red, white, and blue
the one who gave birth to your nation and handed straight
it to you

instead of you patting me on the back
for a job done satisfactorily
you became emboldened by your hatred of me

even though i spent centuries
giving you every part of me

you took my mind
mis-educating me about the history of me

you took my body
through the rape and lynching of me

you took my God
and painted his face to look <u>so</u> unlike me...

and now as my children continue to beg to be free
you send them to the back of the chow line
to prison for at least twenty-five
chains on their hands, their feet,
and even their minds

and every time i turn around
their human rites of passage
are being denied

389 years later
tell me where the hope is
in this here united states of america
where the only thing united is the name.

america: i am

[your mother]   [your father]
[your sister]   [your brother]

[america: i am]

wake up, my people

wake up, my people!

too many of ya'll are still laying there dreaming
dreaming prolific visions for the future, but you're
too stuck on dreaming the dream that you can't even make it
reality

and that's just sad to me.

snap out of it, my people!

wake up and see that the black on your face
is a blessing and <u>not</u> a curse

though that's how they make it seem

it seems like i need to nurse ya'll back to health
to revive the consciousness of the original kings and queens
before you can relinquish
that spirit of victimization
and revolutionize the black masses against westernized
oppression...

wake up, my people!

you have never gotten freedom
off sleeping
your freedom costs too much
for you to be laying there sleeping...
like a baby.

you see, they never stop their hating
that's why they paint you colorful lies of confusion
knowing good and well that the black of your skin
is the key to their extinction
and the trick is

to keep you from believing it

and, everyday, they are making you see
that the black on your face
is a welcome invitation for disaster
reinventing the slave and the master

ask the law enforcement down there in sanford

and anywhere else in america

where whites are continuously <u>pro</u>active
and blacks are continuously <u>re</u>active

we may not be on plantations picking tobacco
but we're still picking cotton
caught-on
caught up on the things that don't matter
not teaching our children to be conscious
so, they lie there unconscious

unconscious of the world around them
unconscious of the history that defines them
unconscious of the red dot on their foreheads
unconscious of the white man's natural desire to kill them,
destroy them, even suffocating their offspring...

and if we don't wake up

Lord, if we don't wake up from this comatose state

the doors of life will close upon us
the nails of the coffin will pound
again and again
<u>never</u> to be reopened
wake up, my people!

shuckin' corn and snappin' peas

deep river

my soul has heard of <u>many</u> rivers
rivers narrow and long – flowing north like the nile -
rivers surging strong and wide – like the ol' mississippi -

rivers rising high and low with the tide
rivers of <u>colored</u> water
crying out from the inside…

"remember me!"
"remember me!"

and i felt my soul crying
tears forming
streaming down my face
like rivers…

rivers of <u>living</u> waters…

the once live living amongst us is
no longer liv…ing…

and this water was no longer living

no longer crystal clear
like the movies make them seem

they're black, brown,
cocoa, mocha
mahogany, cappuccino

- they're colored -

colored waters…

the chilly winds come
breezing vengefully over the waves

(blowing sounds)

and faint sounds of gurgles
gurgling in the distance

bubbles bubbling
at the surface

dark, bloodshot, bulging eyes
staring back at me
over the waters

but wait…

that face looked like a reflection of me
my mother, grandmothers
great grandfathers

oh, God, those eyes
look like the ones that define
my line

ancestrally

from america to alkebulan

kemet is the land that beget me
begot me

and its people are crying out from the colored water
reaching for me.

atlantic/pacific
to be specific
the gulf/artic/indian/
chattahootchie/red/tennessee/
alabama/tallahatchie/mississippi
those rivers have a lot of secrets to dismiss from its lips

beyond till…

i've crossed over the lynch

and i shivered at the thought of all the victims
lurking underneath the bridge
with every inch
my wheels spinned

(wind blowing)

deep river
the secrets of the past
are buried <u>deep</u> beneath the river

in order to progress to our future,

we must…
retrieve … the … anchor!

wade in the water

wade in the water
is what many africans did
post-kidnapping

aboard ships unknown
they were thrown overboard
because their weight was just too massive

bodies slapping hard against the atlantic
and they panicked

vigorously air gasping
their existence soon vanished

so, they waded
for as long as they could
they waded
praying for their kingdom to come
my black people waded

they waded in the water...

time and time again
my people were tired of being punished for
having black skin

they were tired of the whelps and bruises
the rapes and nooses
the black holocaust and the white rule...

so they waded...

from sea to shining sea
they waded...

from dusk to dawn

my people waded...

from 3/5ths of a man to <u>free</u> men
they waded...

the water, you see, was important
it was like Jesus
when He washed away the sins of the world

but <u>this</u> water
washed away the scent of the runaways
got the dogs off their trail
paved the way
for safe escape
to the land of less hate...

and they waded...
they waded...
my people waded...

until they brushed upon the shore
of the land of freedom.

i spit

i spit <u>not</u> for the love of the game
i spit <u>not</u> for the money or the fame
i spit for the many black voices that were tamed
i spit for the many black bodies that were slain in freedom's
name.

i spit for the many african men, women, children
in slave castles of ghana, west africa
who looked out on the atlantic
through "the door of no return"
and never returned.

i spit for every black body that was sold for a bottle of rum.

i spit for every black man whose voice was silenced
when his white master raped his black wife
when his black wife bore master's tan kids
and when his tan stepkids looked at his coal black skin
saying, "nigga, please!"

i spit for every black woman who cried out in tongues of
mother alkebulan for her husband and sons
"kwa bona gala tinaso fa na nay eh!
kwa bona gala tinaso fa na nay eh!"
as they were crucified like Christ
for the betterment of all people
becoming martyrs for our people.

i spit for every
lemuel penn, emmett till, thomas shipp, lamar smith.

i spit for every
virgil lamar ware, medgar evers, james chaney.

i spit for every
johnny robinson, jimmie lee jackson, denmark vesey.

i spit for every
george lee, john reese, henry dee.

i spit for herman dennis middleton, my uncle, who was
killed right here
on these birmingham streets,
october 31, 1963.

i spit because history has left a nasty taste in my mouth
and this is why i spit.

lynching witness

i was there/when!/you hung there/dying./i was there/when!/you
stopped/crying/and nobody can tell me!/just what i was
feeling/that day/mama
came home and told me/that daddy, daddy, daddy, daddy!/was
killed...by lynching.../

i was there

staring up at your
ebony flesh
swinging

here and there
here and there
here and there
here and there
here and there
here and there
here, here
there, there...

the sight was something
i'd never seen

and i'd never heard those
wails

those groans were the
most frightening thing

and i weep

daddy, say it ain't so!

daddy, i was screaming out at the world

in my little girl voice

no! no! that's my daddy!
that's <u>my</u> daddy!!

but

they didn't hear me

they ignored me

shoved me to the ground
like an old rag doll
then they start pulling on his rope

yanking it

yanking it harder

and i just began to call on my Father!

(Father, can you hear me now?)

God, are you there?

i was praying that God would
scream from His omniscient place
and in His almighty voice say,

"free my child! free him!
He's done nothing wrong!"

but He didn't.

and they laughed
fighting over who's gonna get to burn him
who's gonna take his limbs
his legs, his arms, his fingers

oh, my God, they laughed at him.

as he hung there dying.

his eyes bulging.

coughing.   choking.   sweating.

still swinging.

the people singing
all the coon songs
they learned from jim crow.

and i prayed
and i cried

as my daddy died.

for being black
in a sea of whites
laced with a salivating desire
to kill
black men
innocent black men
because of the color of his skin.

friday night fish plates

black on black crime

they say black don't crack, but
black's been cracking since that whip came 'cross our backs

black's been cracking since
afros were still black

black's been cracking
before whitney said 'crack was whack'...

--and may she rest in peace--

and, now, we turn on each other like a barrel full of crabs
straight stealing, killing, destroying everything our
brothers have

jealous of any opportunities up for grabs
so envious you got negroes dying at black hands.

and if i didn't tell you so
there's <u>too many</u> negroes dying at the hands of a black man

so much so that we finally got a job from 'the man'
taken straight from the men in white sheets: the ku klux
klan

and now, they sitting back laughing,
collecting benefits on our behalf

our misplaced anger
got us looking like mad men

naturally

and as time passes
our mentality's crashing

and we accurately know every rhyme
live our lives likewise
as though the rappers didn't fabricate those lines
to make ten dimes

they lying

they didn't do the crime
they didn't do the time
but now our black men standing in the prison line
trying to survive in a masculine, yet rainbow town
acting hard
protecting their behinds...

they're looking at the tv trying to get a feel of the outside
watching foreigners strap bombs on like bras
killing for an unknown cause
but pause...

we kill...just 'cause
just cause some dude looked at us wrong
walked through the 'hood with the wrong color on
folks, we're crippling ourselves!

the blood of their mothers chilled—

stuck singing the same ol' song,
"Lord, why they had to kill <u>my</u> son?

but the heart of the matter is
deep down inside we're angry
we're frustrated
our adrenaline is banging
can't find positive ways to express our anger

we're afraid and live our lives full of fear

we're screaming, but nobody's hearing

we're screaming, but nobody's hearing

-- THE MUSIC IS JUST TOO LOUD! –

disoriented,
we'd rather turn our backs on each other
instead of our real target:
those whose eyes come multicolored

our brains have become so malfunctioned
that we aspire to be our oppressors just too, too much

just to do the things they do, have done
be the people they are and once were

by being criminal to our own kind.

man, blacks gotta stop this black on black crime

get back to back
get black to black
get back to being black

get back to back
get black to black
get back to loving black.

determination of self

"nigger," "nigra," "nigga," even "niggette"
or for the proper folks
"nigress."

they called me colored, nigger boy, savage beast of the field,
uncivilized at best, but
just as i told them,
i'll tell you,

"it's not what you're called,
it's what you ALLOW people to call you."

and i call myself powerful
first born of the most high King,
sister to the Seraphims,
the descendants of those who laid the foundations to the tips
of all of those pyramids.

i am the one whose lineage was christened by the Son,
the one whose roots will live forever through my melanin,

and i keep telling em

"it's not what you're called,
it's what you ALLOW people to call you."

yeah, the "man" beat me down with whips and chains,
enslaved my brain,
whited out my God, & even changed my name…

but deep down inside,
i felt a change a-coming,
i felt a train a-rumbling…

and one day

44

that mental reformation came rushing like a mighty wind, &
it said,

"laquita, the only one who can define you is
the One who gave you definition.
the only who can determine your fate
is the One who determined your beginning."

so, if the person determining your fate, determining your
ability isn't Jesus
then you don't have any business listening.

you see, it's more than just a name.

it's all of the negative connotations with no perforations that
come attached with it.

and if you're not careful,

those subjugated ideologies will fester from gestation
to adolescence
to adulthood
creating another sad generation of self-hating africans in a
lonely nation.

and they say,
"sticks and stones may break my bones, but words will
never hurt me,"

but the truth is,

many of my people have been linguistically annihilated with
racist jargon,
and that's not hardly all,

many of my people have been denied, deprived, contrived,
divested, suppressed, depressed,
with "nigger," "nigra," "nigga"

subconsciously made inferior
never being able to free themselves to see the bigger picture.

and if it's true that "death and life lie in the power of the
tongue,"
then life is what they'll speak whenever <u>my</u> name is
mentioned.

if you allow someone to speak death to your progress
taking your mind as a new age slave,
then you'll be subjugated to others for the rest of your life.

but if you learn to determine your own fate,
then you'll walk alongside kings and queens
with your head held high.

and i, laquita denise middleton-holmes, walk highly!

swing low

swing low, sweet chariot

sometimes i wish someone would swing low &
whisk away the slave mentality of my people,
make them more like my people of the sixties
trying hard to be seen with dignity
yet, dying by the boatloads demanding, "give us free!"

i wish that chariot so sweet would swoop down and
carry us back to a time when niggas weren't your friends,
just everyone with black skin
or black kin,
back skin ripped open with massa's whip,
middle name boy, first name nigger,
negro don't you know that
"nigger" was equivalent to being intellectually ignorant?

banned from education they kept niggas limited,
caught trying to read niggas lost their hands, even fingers!

& now we use "nigga" to define our friendships,
our kinships

but let it seep from white lips
& see how white lips turn into
the big, black, and bloody red lips of a minstrel!
then we scream she's racist!
he's prejudiced!
when our only claim to fame is to
achieve power by using the white man's game.

to that i say,

swing low, sweet chariot, coming for to carry me home...!

man, we need to get our minds right.
it ain't all about black and white,

it's about a balance of power

yeah, put that on your timeline,
give it a beat & make it a ringtone,
put it in a mixtape,
& sell it out your trunk & call it "black tape."
we dying anyway,

call caution to the wind, there's been a genocide,
no, a mass suicide, of original kings & queens,
broken halos,
and ripped up wings.

and the sad thing is…

they didn't know…

they didn't even know they were fashioned in an image
called His…

their minds just consumed with beats & rhythms…
illegal facts & figures…
carry the key to the kingdom…
so true to the 'hood they'd rather stay niggas…

dang…

swing low, sweet chariot!
coming for to carry me home.

swing low, sweet chariot
coming for to carry me home.

the mystification of the new negro

i remember when we were an innovative people...
a naturally creative people

when the rest of the world stole our ideas
and ran with them

now, we're so comfortable in our position,
we say to hell with it.

none of our stuff now is original.
the main focus is the almighty benjamin.
confused
we're siding with the enemy
as they steadily destroying and killing us.

stealing every vein of us...

while we shake and gyrate
hate and titillate ourselves
we laugh it off like "whatever nigga!"

not comprehending the damage of being erased from history
with the very blood of our existence
being nonexistent...

steada being over persistent
we worry ourselves with matters that are trivial:

how big our rims is
how tight our m&m, 7 up, marvin the martian cars is
with no official endorsement deals
not even a letter making it official.

ya'll people are pitiful!

you still living in the projects with your auntee's sister

eating up her food out of her kitchen
talking 'bout some, "stop snitchin!"

chile, u need to stop niggering!

dead (black) man walking

he's a dead man walking
walking to the down beat of his own drum
trying to find his way in this world
with no direction
no help from the population

so, they leave him to survive on his own
and he's lonely

and at every moment
he's knocked down on another notch on
the old totem pole

the prison's calling his name
and they're waiting for him to answer...

and they're impatient

so, they lock him away on fraudulent charges
give him twice the time
for the same crime
'cause they know no one is gonna miss him

'cept his mama

and she's gathering her life savings
and her prayer warriors together
praying for a miracle
fasting for his deliverance

not even <u>he</u> knows the only one who can deliver him
is Jesus...

because he's a dead man walking
walking to the down beat of his own drum
ducking and dodging his conscience

his heart and very essence is syncing up to
the same drum and they go,

"ho hum, ho hum, ho hum…"

he's so disillusioned
he doesn't look in the mirror

so, he doesn't notice the target on his head

and they're waiting for the right time to strike

be it day or night
as long as it's before he turns 25

he doesn't value his life
so he lives for death

death by suicide is the new mass genocide
claiming the lives
of those who live their lives by the dollar
and by the gun

and that's why most of our sons
are dead men walking

walking right into the hangman's noose
walking down to the end of the dock
right up to the guillotine
right up to the new age auction block

and before you know it
they're SOLD!

sold out to the man
sold out to the stereotypes
sold out to the things that plagued our men
since before we got here

becoming statistics without even knowing it

and it's just a shame.

that he is the most dominant force in this whole human race
and he doesn't even know his place.

he's just a dead man walking.

negro of the suburbs

it kills me

it kills me
how easily we forget the struggles of the past
forget the ones who brought freedom to pass
forget the sacrifices, the struggles, and everything else...

and now, we just sit back and laugh...

and it kills me

to see these people who think freedom came free

--even Jesus had to die to give freedom to me--

and just few short years ago
many a black folks swung to and fro
on that same wood that Jesus hung on
and others

billie sang of the poplar ones
that carried the blood stains of our ancestors' brothers
and uncles and cousins, even mothers

and ya'll still think this freedom came free!

and it kills me

because centuries later,
we're <u>still</u> fighting to break the chains of slavery

you see, every time we drive in the wrong side of town,
we're profiled
every time we shop in the wrong chain stores, we're spied
every time we date the right people in the wrong color
we end up hanging up from the same trees
as our mother's brothers

and it kills me
how dr. maya said, "we are the hope of the slave"
yet, we don't know his story

our blackness we ignore
from the dark skin to the afro
and just because i *boldly go*
where few blacks ever go
doesn't mean i'm unattractive because i am proud to let
my naps show.

and it kills me

how we worry ourselves with issues that are trivial
instead of the things that are pivotal
to our people's upliftment.

many of our people fought, bled, and died
for equal access to education,
but today our kids can't read

many of our people fought, bled, and died
for equal access to public accommodations
but today our kids would rather sit at the back of the bus—
than to make rosa parks' dream a reality.

many of our people fought, bled, and died
for equal access at the voting booth
but today our kids only vote when the candidate is black.

many of our people fought, bled, and died
for equal access to life and livelihood
but today our kids don't give a crap about that.

many of our people fought, bled and died
for equal access in department stores
but today our kids are raised to be consumers---

not entrepreneurs.

they're decked out in the newest gear,
but can't read the label
and it's our fault
because we continuously enable them.

we were groomed as a village
now, we're several houses on a street
everyone wants to be an individual
failing to realize the power in UNITY

we ignore the call of racial responsibility
steadily crabbing everybody back to the barrel
keeping other negros from having
what we don't have.

and it kills me.

freedom piece

freedom
liberty
emancipate
this proclamation
and set... my... people... free

free their minds
so, ignorance won't consume their souls

free their spirits
so, their zest for freedom will never grow old

ol' willie did a number on our people
lynching not only black bodies
but also our black temples

putting dimples
in our thoughts and beliefs
and called himself friendly

pitted us against each other like enemies

for centuries

and now we despise each other
like negros ain't kin to me

and you

sucking up to the white man like his friendship is true

that whole

"if you're white/you're right"

is what we hold true

breastfeed to our children and
set it as the foundation of the things we knew
and know

when it was just a short time ago
he placed us in the back of the bus
the streetcar, the train

we rode on that freedom bus as
he beat us with billy clubs to the brain

ask john lewis, jim peck, jim zwerg
forget what you read
it's about what you heard
and hearing

they won't teach you this in the educational system!

told us we weren't good enough to drink his water
though it came from the same drain
gased us like exterminators
on that selma to montgomery trail

bombed our beloved churches--even on christmas
had our kids dodging dogs & water--& not even missing

we
my people,
need to stop asking permission
and start making decisions
on <u>our</u> future

and that of our children

because the longer we wait
the longer we suffer
and frankly,

i don't have the time

<u>we</u> don't have the time.

and we are tired.
like fannie lou hamer said,

chile, "i'm tired of being sick and tired."

tired of the perception of my race
determining my place
in society

tired of my people relinquishing their power
because they think they have none

and i don't know who you came from
but i came from the <u>Almighty</u>

the <u>lone</u> omnipotent

and if i'm His kid
then no one on <u>His</u> given earth
can take away or give me
my freedom.

we need you

my people,
we need you to stand up
no, not just for an award
as the crowd is clapping and praising you
with the cameras clicking, taking pictures of you

we need you to <u>be</u> the change we need in this world

we need you to <u>be</u> the men who take charge of
our young men
<u>giving</u> them positive examples to look up to
<u>being</u> the positive examples they look up to

so, their minds can conceptualize careers --
and not just jobs

so, their minds can conceptualize a world outside
of the 'hood --
and not just dealing on the block

so, their minds can conceptualize themselves as leaders --
and not just followers
following every trend the world has to offer:
like drugs, the booze, the women
fancy cars, fast cash, and fast dreams
that lead them to straight to either
the 1) cemetery or the 2) penitentiary.

you see, we need you to help educate these young men
on how to love themselves enough to love others:
their women, their mothers
the children they donated time and energy to
<u>before</u> conception,
but for some reason fail to continue
post-delivery

we need you to help them see other options
than to kill their sisters and brothers

-- in cold blood --

we're supposed to be our brothers' keepers,'
but yet their blood is crying out too often from the ground
and the collective sound is just too, too loud for the living

and, instead of making us whole,
it takes away the very sustenance that helps
keep our people alive

and, no, i just cannot bear another
"justifiable homicide."

we need you to help them see their self-worth
so, they can make a positive impact on this earth

we need you to help them become the men future
generations read about in admiration
like we do dr. king, du bois, and mr. douglass during slavery

we need you to help them set goals for themselves
and attain them

we need you to help them transition from
the little boys mentality to a grown man's mentality

so, when their little boys grow up
their teachings of manhood will come from their daddy,
and not from a loc'ed out rapper
who doesn't even live half the life he glorifies in his raps

we need you to help them transition from
the little boys mentality to a grown man's mentality

so, when their little girls grow up

their teaching of womanhood will not include her
surrendering her integrity
for fast cash, love, and acceptance
from little boys posing as men
exploiting her at every chance he gets
laughing at her expense.

Proverbs 22:6 says to "train up a child in the way
he should go, and when he is old he will not depart from it,"
but the problem is
the older generation has stopped passing on the knowledge
we desperately need for survival...

and without that,
we perish.

so, now, i beseech you, my brethren to stand up

no, not just for an award
as the crowd is clapping and praising you
with the cameras clicking, taking pictures of you

we need you to <u>be</u> the change we need in this world

don't just simply add it to your trophy case
or hang it on your home's wall of fame.

take it as a baton passed to you in a relay race.

those men before you have run their distance well
and, now, it's your turn use all of your
training, experience, & expertise
to advance us to the next generation of runners
who'll take your teachings,
mix it with their experiences
and raise up another group of runners
who are strong,
full of endurance, and

determined enough
to get our people closer to the finish line.

my people
we need you.

silly of me

it was silly of me to think that i
could ever save a whole race of folk
with my mind
the stroke of my pen
the typeset of my pc

must have been a joke from me
to think that i
could ever emancipate my people
from mental slavery

must have been foolish of me to
think that i
bore the same hope
as the slave
possessed the same courage
to shuttlesworth God gave

must—have—been—out—of—my—e-ver—bles-sed—mind
to think that i
could ever lead my people out of bondage
through an angry white sea
parting way to give us free –
dumb of me
to think that maybe—

--maybe--

i'd be that person to actually dedicate my life
liberating a people who didn't know they were bound

resurrecting the unknowing dead from the ground

loosening the shackles from their brains
and freeing their minds…

oh, yes, it must be silly of me
just like it must have been for dr. king,
gandhi, martin luther,
toussaint l'ouverture
before they saved many of their people
bound by oppression
depression,
suppression,
and i'm just guessing
that many of their peers considered them
ludicrous, fruitless, even stupid
for doing things that their own
fear wouldn't let them do

silly of me to think that i
am just as needed as nat turner,
mr. prosser, mr. vesey
yes, many have called me crazy
for contesting female subjugation
like susan b. and elizabeth cady
they be understanding the need for female equality
against sexist iniquity.

born black and female
i'm at the bottom of the totem pole
though my days are not old
i've been told i have an old soul

and right now
my soul's been crying out for my people
i'd ride or die for my people

--and the time is now--

for us to take control over our lives,
our situations, our future generations

and if it takes me being labeled as "silly"

then silly be me
the power be within me
the power be within the people

all hail the power of the people!

sistahs don't swim

dark is lovely

in the younger years
black girls were taught
beauty was only in the
white dolls mama bought

long, straight blonde hair
in bows & pigtails
school paper skin was the subliminal
yearning of all young females

who could ever forget
that long, thin nose & those almost non-existent lips
this was the epitome of beauty
no one ever told us we were being jipped

subconsciously, we learned that
we were inferior; we were ugly
not even blacks believed that
being dark was lovely.

inadvertently, we learned to hate ourselves
and love our oppressors
self-hatred consumed us & was
passed on to our successors.

then comes the experience
of being dark versus being light
although we were all black
only being light was considered "right".

psychologically, we were battered
into hating our darker halves
whites divided & conquered us
now, they're admiring the madness they created
with a coke and a laugh.

black **and** beautiful

i'm beautiful.
<u>not</u> to be dark,
but because i am

~beautiful~

and i love me <u>and</u> who i am
because if i don't who will?

my beauty comes naturally.
not plastically.

and to be created this great,
one has to be begotten from greatness,
the greatest.
the Creator.

not to mention that beautiful black man and woman
who made me.

and lately
i been thinking about the things that lace me
beautifully.

and all the hateful things people have said
to make me hate me.
like,

"why is your skin <u>so</u> dark?"

i just respond,"it's because i've been kissed by the sun."

and if you think about it
across africa lies the equator…

--right where my ancestors came from—

they say they can't understand why
i'm happy to be nappy
even say they dread seeing my dreadlocks,
but
i dread it <u>just so</u> you can dread it

lock it in its natural form
just so
when you look upon me
you have no question of where my people come from

and in case you don't remember,
my level of melanin won't let you forget it!

some even have the nerve to say,
"that girl was left in the oven too long!"

but i simply say,

"nah, i was just cooked to perfection!"

they say i'm arrogant
even say i'm vain,
but i invite you to take an imaginary trip with me

and just imagine

can you imagine just how many more successful
little black girls we'd have
if people would've told them of their beauty
at a young age?

can you imagine
how many bad choices they would not have made
if they were laced with the self-confidence
to go beyond any player line a man would tell?

i dare you to imagine

a world full of powerful black women
standing proud and sure
with hopes and dreams for the future,
who are raising positive-minded, self-determined

black girls
who don't cry out loud in the dark

black girls
who have <u>not</u> considered suicide when the rainbow was
enuf...

black girls
who look to God and not men when the going gets tough...

black girls
black girls
black girls
beautiful black girls
who set their own pace
stare adversity in its face
and laugh hysterically
when it tries to claim her place.

so, from here on
i will continue to say i'm beautiful
my daughters are beautiful
my sistahs are beautiful
my aunts are beautiful
my mom and grandmom are beautiful

and they are
a reflection of me
and i of them
and together, we stand as the
epitome of black beauty.

nappy hair

not to sound sappy
but i like to wear my hair nappy
free of perms, relaxers,
the heat of straightening combs...
too reminiscent of hot days under the master...

if you want me to be happy
style my hair in no way but nappy

give me a scoop of ether nine
locs or twists, either's fine
don me an 'angela'...

before you open your mandible
i'll tell ya the world judges you by the tangible

my hair is a physical representation of my beliefs
so, you'll have a little inkling about me--**before** i begin to
speak

my sista, my nappy roots go all the way back
to the land of kings & queens who were sun-kissed so black
to queen cleo & queen nefertiti
to linguists espousing history in the pyramids of egypt

but...
let me bring it back
to why i like my kitchen black
with dark, hazy, smoky naps...

it reminds me of all my grannies
raped, abandoned,
kidnapped to a land where their fannies
determined their worth
how many miscegenated babies

they could birth
as she increased in girth
she became known as the
black mother earth
breastfeeding the white child on the right tit
her mulatto one on the left
feeding the master his bacon & grits
while her fellow slaves ate what was left of it.

when i say i love my naps in the back
it's truly because i love 'em like that.

no color, no dye
no reason to fry...

but i guess the white southerners say so
so they hanged my forefathers on trees for public show
auctioning off body parts to be placed on mantles
seeing my forefathers' 'parts' in a jar for candles
is way <u>too</u> much for my new age soul to handle...

some say freedom ain't free
but how much freedom can you have
dangling lifelessly from a tree?

my hair...is a daily visual reminder that
my people persisted
in the wake of severe resistance.

whites burned the cross
while blacks bore the cross.

whites hid their faces
while we flaunted ours desegregating public places

in the name of GOD they killed
by the name of GOD we lived...

so, when i say i love being black
& i love all the slinky kinks in the back
it's because there's so much history wrapped up
in every single coil of my naps.

my black history

the sounds of kenya forever ring in my ear
when i saunter down the street
i have no fear
my hips go a-swaying to the beat of the wind
and gives only a hint of the woman within.

my native nigeria calls out through my big brown eyes
and causes my dark, angelic cheek bones to rise
as i continue my journey to the unknown guile
i cause a frictionous revolution between my thick thighs

then down, down, on my dark brown
does my strong mighty hands begin to frown
upon the thought of centuries of hard labor this red, white,
& blue
forced upon my forefathers and foremothers. yes, it's true

these europeans were on a mission
to erase my formal traditions, saying,
"hey, darkie!!! abort your language and talk like me
take those baskets off your heads & walk like me!!!"

now that i am in america—known as an "african-
american"—
what am i supposed to do with all the things that made me
african?
am i supposed to give up what my forefathers taught me,
and forget the land from where the europeans brought me?

no, i will lift my powerful and commanding hands to the sky
and i will tell the entire universe why
i continue to walk around with my head held high
and why my eyes will forever be fixed upon the prize.

it is because the love of my native africa lives

within my soul and shines brightly through my smile. it
gives
me the strength to survive in a country that has always
hated me,
abated me, and systematically placed me in the category of
subjugation—
they'd even call me a nigger to my face.

no matter what land i live in or the harshness that i have to
withstand
nothing will ever force me to give up on my native land.

eulogy

she said she would stay

"i will stay with you
through the ups and the downs…"

as he went up and down the sides of her face
she bowed her head and cried

"yes, i will stay with you
when no one else is around"

as he claimed bouts of infidelity and lies
she prayed in her head "God, why?"

"and when the dark clouds arise
i will stay by your side."

she remembered the vows she made to love him through it
all
no matter how bad the stormy weather
in her heart she knew they'd always stay together

"and i know we'll be alright
i will stay with you."

but never
did she quite imagine
that he'd tear through her vaginal
walls over and over again
with a rapist's pleasure
a predator's joy

and all she could remember
was screaming prayers in her velvet-lined sheets
and her voice growing silent

as no one seemed to hear her

never
would they believe he'd cause her pain like this.

no, not the infamous
sergeant vincent ellis.

and after every time
he wiped her eyes
and apologized
promising "no more"

so, she loved him
once more

and once more he
took his frustrations out on her face
full fisted, full frontal

"no, supervisor, i wasn't hit.
it was just one of my clumsy accidents."

but her supervisor knew
passed her a card
saying,
"mrs. ellis, these people
can help you."

before she could leave
a well of tears formed.

before then
she thought she was normal.

she thought she had it all together.

but the whelps on her body

became more and more evident
and she became even more hesitant
about being the strong woman
she alluded to the public
she was.

for some reason
all of her power seemed to diminish
the moment he started speaking...

he controlled her every move
most importantly her mind

he didn't have to say one word
for her to walk that line

because she knew
once they were behind closed doors

she would again become his victim

and once more
he would apologize

but <u>this</u> time
that once more

is no more.

eulogy of anita lynne parker-ellis,
attorney at law, mother of one,
dead at 28.

God of the Hebrews (11:1)

black Jesus

when my dark day comes
let me die a black Jesus
for my people

let me die a martyr
for my people

let me carry my cross to gethsemane
just like Jesus did
all in the name of His people

-- and they called Him black Jesus --

they beat Him
lash after lash
they spat on Him

as He prayed for them and healed them
they laughed at Him

-- a good laugh --

and as they whipped Him
not once did He ever ask His Father to stop them
nor send His angels down to protect His
only ... begotten ... Son ...

they adorned His head with thorns
laughing, hahaha!

sparing the guilty, but torturing the innocent

<u>still</u> He declared,
"Father, forgive them for they know not what they do."

but their actions fulfilled prophecy.

and "greater love hath no man than this
that a man lay down his life for his friends."

and He laid it down
just like the old testament prophets said He would.
and when i close my eyes to eternal rest
i want this verse
to describe my life the best.

i want to be like my black Jesus
who carried the torch
without losing the fi-yah
just so my people could live eternally
in eternity, freely in society

when my dark day comes
drape my long, woolly hair
along my shoulders;
let my brow face the east
so, i can look upon the prince of peace.

let the people look upon me for i am comely.
and as the sky turns black
let them look upon me
and see that
<u>black</u>. <u>is</u>. <u>beautiful</u>.

let them remember
my supernatural conviction
to uplift and better my people

how divine intervention placed me in the right place
at the right time
to continue the legacy of those who lived and died
in the struggle

let them revive the memory
of all my people

sold on the auction block,
those who took up arrow & bow
even as the rifles cocked.

let them know that i lived my life
telling the stories
of all my people
who ran for their freedom
in the middle of the night
who never lost their zest for dignity
as they were whipped, beaten, trying to be free

lash after lash
Lord, they laughed, hahaha!
those white people laughed
as black bodies burned in the daylight

let my people remember that i gave my very existence
stayed persistent
insistent on freeing them from their mental captivities
advancing them socially, economically,
spiritually...

and as the little children hear stories of
revolutionaries
let my name be in the midst of the list.

let them know that i first served as a visionary
envisioning a better future than our past
igniting a new millennium revolution destined to bear good
fruit.

let me live my life to bring hope to my people
that they will not look upon their past
as a distant one

for it is the very past that provides the
sustenance that maintains us in the present

and provides us the compass that leads us to our future.

let them know that together we are
the seed of the first adam,
the second one, too.

we are the seed of those african kings
and queens whose intellectual capabilities
stimulated the entire earthly realm.

and upon their shoulders they have all built this rock
and we shall stand upon it together.

and live in the honor of the one and only
black Jesus.

testimony

dear Heavenly Father,

Lord, as i stand here amongst these doubting thomases
i'm reminded of how far You done brought us

i know the devil preys on those whose faith is weak
but, Lord, i ain't got to question You
because You already answered me!

Your Word says, "now faith is the substance of things hoped
for,
the evidence of things not seen."

and although i'm only 25,
down through my years, i done seen You being good to me!

so, never in my life will i ever begin to doubt Your power
because every single time i cried out in despair,
You came and saved me from my darkest hour.

when i laid there freezing cold without a home
on these birmingham streets
Lord, You wrapped me in the cradle of Your arms giving me
heat.

when i laid there on that surgeon's bed
& the doctor took knife to head
Lord God, <u>You</u> said
"...thou shalt not die until My purpose for <u>you</u> is fulfilled."

and 3 years later, God, hallelujah, i'm still tumor-free!

when my child's father sucked the living soul out of me
leaving me without a breath
Lord God, You came down from Your Heavenly post
& saved me from a fate worse than death.

so, never in my life will i ever begin to doubt Your power
because every single time i cried out in despair,
You came and saved me from my darkest hour

and that's why today i sing, "can't nobody do me like Jesus!"
and can't nobody tell me You ain't been good to me!

sermon: enemy, you don't have a hold on me!

*The LORD is my light and my salvation; whom shall I fear? the
LORD is the strength of my life; of whom shall I be afraid? -
Psalms 27:1*

i've seen many a trials in my day
some you may not believe and some you may

i've had enemies rise up against me in full demonic anger
but the Lord God of Hosts said, "no! she's <u>My</u> child and do
her no danger!"

and you know when God speaks,
even the king of the jungle has to bow in complete
obedience.

when God speaks,
even the power of the royal kingdom in england has to be
relinquished.

you see,
God spoke the whole world into existence
He's omnipresent, omniscient, omnipotent!

and if you don't believe me,
walk on out upon that water
and stay afloat

even Jesus' beloved Peter
didn't have the power to stand
without believing in the Father of Jesus!

you see,
i've seen the enemy rise right up out of his master's domain
without the pitchfork and the horns that hollywood
proclaims

just simple ol' negroes
in regular clothes
overtaken by the evil spirit of their fallen leader

and if you don't believe me,
open your Bibles to ephesians 6:12 where it says,

"for we wrestle not against flesh and blood,
but against powers and principalities and the rulers of darkness."

maybe one, maybe two
but most times many
that they call "legion."

plotting and scheming
trying to cut a deal
on <u>my</u> soul

but the Lord didn't deem that to be so!

He said,
"this is <u>MY</u> child of whom I'm well pleased."
just like He said to Jesus
as John lifted Him from that *deep river...*

and just like God told Satan in the matters of Job
you can do whatever you will
but today, tomorrow, and forever
only to Me will she kneel

and He was right.

because i was raised by those old women deep down south
who taught me what king david said,

"i once was young and now i am old; yet have i not seen the
righteous forsaken,

nor His seed begging bread."

i knew God would <u>never</u> leave me
i knew He would always set His angels encamp all around
me
i knew He would always put a protective hedge around me
just like those old women prayed

and as the enemy got close
taking aim
they got caught up in their own snares

--you know the ones they set for me--

you may not know it, yet,
but God saved me for a greater purpose
just like He told Jeremiah in Jeremiah 1:5

*"before I formed thee in the belly I knew thee; and before thou
camest forth out of the womb I sanctified thee, and I ordained thee
a prophet unto the nations."*

i come today to tell you that i may not be up on the
mountaintop
preaching to all the world

i may not have a congregation of thousands upon ten
thousands
worshipping God in spirit and in truth

i may not have my name in bright lights selling out
coliseum after coliseum, but

i know that God has a purpose for me and His people
just like it's said in Ecclesiastes 3:1,

"To every thing there is a season, and a time to every purpose under the heaven"

and we must know that God's will <u>will</u> be done
"on earth
as it is in Heaven"

--just like we teach the kids to pray--

and not a devil in hell,

--nor the ones roaming the earth--

can stop the power of God
from manifesting His will
through His chosen vessel!

enemy, you don't have a hold on me!

the doors of the church are open.

do you remember?

last night i had a dream

it was a very peculiar dream…

one full of omens
and cautions and warnings and things…

the Heavenly gates slowly closed
and there knelt a man begging, weeping
pleading for his eternity

as the Angel proceeded to close the book,
the man became so emotional,
that the Angel called upon the master of the house:
God, Himself.

when the man saw God, he began to plead his case.
fighting through his tears he said,

"God, i know you caught me when i was out there running
the streets,
acting like the world was created by me.

i admit i did some wild and crazy things
but, God, you HAVE to have mercy on me!

this world, <u>YOU</u> created, is a very sinful place
full of idols and adultery
thieving and murdering

sin is glorified in the music
the tube, magazines, and books
affecting all ages,
from the old folks to the babies, too.

God, i know i fell into the way of the world

indulging in those things that weren't in Your will
not stopping to think i was hurting You—until

that day You called my name
calling me in to love You
to live for You, to do the things You wanted me to.

do you remember Lord?
do you remember?

Lord, i remember learning Your Word,
even learning that that voice inside me was Yours i heard.

Lord, i went to church most sundays
prayed at the altar, fellowshipped, and got baptized
even paying my offering, building fund, and my tithes

but i'll admit, after while
my ways on the other days
led me astray.

Lord, i mean, in my heart i wanted to live for You, but
this world YOU created was just too crazy to be faithful to
You

everywhere you turn, there is sin and evil
permeating the atmosphere
the only place of escape is here in the stratosphere.

Lord, You just <u>HAVE</u> to understand…

[God:]
yes, I remember my child
when you hung with the wild…
when you hurt Me by ignoring My calls
even when you knew I sent My Son to die for you all.

yes, I remember my little one

when you were out there indulging in your sinful fun,
when you forgot all about ME &
all those blessings I continuously gave thee.

yes, I remember when I sent all the saints of My church
to remind you that you needed to do My work
only to have you shun them away
just so you could continue in your sinful ways.

yes, My child, I remember every single day of your life
even before <u>AND</u> afterwards.

I remember every time you came to Me in desperate need,
only to have you turn away even when I gave unto you
freely.

yes, child, I remember all of those things and more
but now as you stand before My gates of Heaven without a
clue

I have to proclaim the words I do remember saying,

"child, since you never knew Me, I never knew you."

chocolate-covered sushi

rev. fred shuttlesworth, christmas 1956

they bombed his house as
his children opened presents.
christmas means nothing.

day of dawning: 9/15/63

september fifteenth
birmingham was calvary
six children martyred.

emmett louis till

he was a young child
wanted to make mama proud
coffin left open.

everyday black

not twenty-eight days...
i can't escape this black face--
it stays everyday.

i love me-lanin

why wear nappy hair?
to show the melanin-less
i love melanin.

black mo(u)rning

one black morning
her breath stuck. wide eyes bucked
the moment he died.

journey from swine

ain't no sunshine

freedom—
something that we, new age negroes, take for granted.

quickly—
we forget how our ancestors lost their lives so we
could sit at any lunch counter
in the front of the bus &
could be called something more positive than 'nigger'

now—
we walk around like our ancestors weren't slaves
who were hung on trees
like pigs ready for slaughter
who were whipped into bleeding--
until their backs were welted into gashes
of hurt, of anger,
of the things that brought them so much suffering...
yeah, we forget about that.

we forget about the countless number of
days, months, years, decades, centuries
our ancestors had to slave in the tobacco & cotton fields
in all the heat of the day...
beckoning to their master's every call
even the calls that claimed all
of our women's dignity,
honor,
& respect.

oh, yeah, we forget about that.

we forget about the 13th, the 15th, and the 19th amendments
ending slavery and establishing the right to vote

we forget about the state officials blocking the entrances
to the schools that offered the most.

we forget about birmingham's police trained dogs
and high pressure water hoses

we forget about the 3,000 + children going to jail singing,

"i ain't gon let nobody turn me 'round
i ain't gon let bull connor turn me 'round
i ain't gon let segregation turn me 'round…"

we forget about the sting of tear gas in hopeful voters' eyes
on the road from selma to montgomery

we forget about the unjust jail sentences
that claimed the lives of so many of our
innocent freedom fighting people.

nobody ever wants to remember the past,
but i'll tell you that
ain't no sun gon' shine
in our lives until we realize that our history
is too deep to be lost in a world of
trivial pursuits.

when we forget the journeys of our ancestors
ain't no sun gon' shine

when we fail to learn our true history
ain't no sun gon' shine

when we fail to teach our children
ain't no sun gon' shine

my people
don't let the non-remembrance of our history
be the cause of our downfall.
don't let our history die away.

footsteps

all i could hear was footsteps

marching … nonstop

like soldiers marching up to the front lines
synchronized

time after time
these footsteps sounded loudly
every step pounding,
freedom!   freedom!   freedom!   freedom!

simply begging for a piece of the pie called "equal."

in the middle of the night
i heard footsteps tiptoeing
through the fields
over hills
marching towards that bright, northern star

seemed so far
but, yet, it was so close

i even heard footsteps wading the waters of the great ohio

on a trail dubbed the underground railroad
conducted by a lady moses

where roses weren't made for black people
<u>before</u> the ruling of "separate, but equal"
my people wanted
freedom!   freedom!   freedom!   freedom!

and they marched
treading the path of righteousness for freedom's sake

and they marched
deep in the hidden floors and attics of those quakers

and they marched
382 days all across the city of montgomery

and they marched
until their freedom on paper mirrored their realities

and they marched
three times in selma '65, fifty four miles

and they marched
day in and day out just to utilize their voting rights

and they marched
up on the steps of the lincoln memorial

and they marched
'cause they knew which god was holding 'em

and they marched
to city halls downtown and department stores

and they marched
n.a.a.c.p., a.c.m.h.r., s.c.l.c., s.n.c.c., and core

and they marched
even when their feet were bloody, blistered, and sore
even when their feet were bloody, blistered, and sore
even when their feet were bloody, blistered, and sore

and because they marched

i am here.

we are here.

they shouldn't have let me taste freedom

they shouldn't have let me taste freedom.

should've left me in the back of the colored section
up in the balcony
in the back seats
still begging to be free.

they should've left me thriving off colored water
no, they shouldn't have bothered
to let me near their children in school
letting my blackness intrude
on their children's lily white mentalities
creating fallacies
on the things they thought they knew...

no, they shouldn't have let me taste freedom
because it's just like chicken
and i want to indulge in it in every single way

died, fried, laid to the side
baked, caked, castrated

i want freedom like watermelon

succulent, red, grown in hot places
on the front porch all over my black face.

no, i don't think they should've let me taste freedom
because the spirits of my revolutionary fathers blaze
through my eyes
like panthers—black—
and i'd like to see them take freedom from NAT

no, he wouldn't have that!

what about my fireblazing mothers

who endured murder, familial separation,
forced miscegenation
humiliation
on a daily basis

i would like to see the day
harriet became re-enslaved

we wouldn't even know white people existed
in this age.

and as i speak from the african side of me
the seminole and cherokee
kicks and screams
begging to be free

no, ma'am, we shouldn't have let those white faces off those
boats

we should've taken arrows and bows to their throats
until they choked

coached them right back onto those boats
oh, pinta,
oh, maria,
we should've sent them back screaming for Jesus!

no, we shouldn't have believed them.

our new friends???
man, please!

they came
discovered our land already found
turned around
and tried to tie us down
as slaves
but we didn't play

we matched their murder
with massacre
the sight of their blood
didn't deter our desire
to maintain what was rightfully ours

and, yeah, many of our people died
and we cried
as we traveled the trail of tears
while conquering our fears
we died
inside
when they took our whole land
and narrowed it down to just one state

yeah, we hated it, but
we equaled the slate
with this thing called cas-I-nos
and now they bottoms up like whinos

bring all their money, their lives
giving it to the ones
they tried to cause full demise to
and for that, we love you,

so, drink,
be merry,
bring us <u>all</u> your fruit
because your fruit
makes our trees grow
fruitfully.

so, yes, i'll take my freedom with kool-aid, <u>all</u> red

take it as you may,
but i'd be dead sleeping in my grave
before i be somebody's slave!

because now that i've tasted freedom
i'll fight to the death of the world
to protect the freedoms of my little girls.

nah, they shouldn't have let me taste freedom!

salutations of a visionary

and i salute
barack hussein obama

because when many people said he couldn't
he said, "yes we can!"
and we believed him.

"yes we can!"
was heard like the gunshot that killed dr. king
it was heard all over the world
and we screamed it loud and clear,

"YES WE CAN!" (3xs)

i looked down to mexico and i heard the spanish saying,
"!PODEMOS SI!" (3xs)

i looked to paris, france and i heard the french saying,
"OUI NOUS POUVONS!" (3xs)

i looked down in kenya and i heard the kenyans crying out,
"YES WE CAN!" (3xs)

you know,
i even looked over to russia and i heard the russians saying,
"да мы можем" *(3xs)*

but this gunshot was louder than that.

they said it sounded like the sound of the wall of berlin
falling...
better yet, i think it sounded like the sound of the walls of
jericho falling.

it sounded like the sound of Gabriel's horn calling so,

Gabriel blow your horn
blow your horn Gabriel

it sounded like the sound of Jesus, the Christ,
ascending to Heaven.

and, wow, doesn't Heaven feel nice…

and for the millions of whites who have historically told us
to "wait"

the wait is over!

and now, we are reaping the fruits of our ancestors'
backbreaking labor.

and, oh, doesn't this manna from Heaven taste good?
mmm mmm!!!
this manna tastes <u>so</u> good…

240,000 people gathered in that
freezing grant park
to witness him reach a once unattainable landmark.

on november 4, 2008,
he became a legend
with God in all His glory smiling down from Heaven,
saying, "you are My son with whom I am well pleased."

and, yes, we were all well-pleased
with a man who dared to stand upon footsoldiers' shoulders
making reality of their fantasies…
not just parks and king
but all of those soldiers seen and unseen.

we were all well-pleased
with a man who overcame
all of america's obstacles

to become the most logical
candidate for america's presidency
establishing full residency
at 1600 pennsylvania avenue

where just a few years ago,
he would've only served "the man" with slave gratitude,
a subservient attitude,
but now he's the man making all the rules.

and, wow, doesn't that feel good?!

then there's january 20, 2009
the day that'll be forever etched in time
when he successfully crossed that line
that minorities were never supposed to cross

--he bore that cross--
believing in america when it lost faith in itself

--he bore that cross--
believing in himself when only his family did

--he bore that cross--
having the audacity to hope outside the box,
beyond that glass ceiling,
outside those stereotypes that kept us bowing and kneeling.

he restored within the world a new feeling of the possibility
that change... could truly... come to america

making it truly the "land of the free
and the home of the brave."

not of those enslaved and those who live in fear.

behold:

a new day is here
change has finally come to america.

i've walked with kings and queens

i've walked with kings and queens

i've walked with kings and queens
those who blazed the trail
and those whose torches gleamed

i've entertained civil rights movement royalty
to learn the stories of those who preceded me...

emmitt louis till

and i give reverence to
emmitt louis till

because when he died
my whole family cried.

they wondered how they could lynch a mother's only son
for allegedly being a mannish one?

for a long time after his body was found,
his voice haunted black folk from the muddy ground, saying

"don't let them deny me justice,
don't let my death be in vain
let it be the impetus for ensuring this won't happen again

for the south is a cruel one
--too different than the north--
whatever you do,
don't let love & justice divorce..."

sojourner truth

and i give reverence to
sojourner truth

who traveled the lands far and wide
spreading truth

when whites professed violence
she spoke out when women were supposed to be silent

she spoke louder when blacks were annihilated
nightly
and daily

and daily she advocated equal rights
for blacks and women, she knew a change was coming
when she delivered "ain't i a woman?"

preaching that if she could do the same thing as a man
why should she be treated differently...

if we are all divinely made,
why should we be treated differently?

malcolm x

and i give reverence to
malcolm x

who led the fight under the nation of islam
teaching that blacks were royalty,
teaching black identity
not in the context of whites,
but in the context of the world

originally, he believed in the separatist thought
that blacks should create a nation within a nation
with our own schools that would teach true education
of who we are, who we were, and who we would become.

originally, he believed that whites were blue-eyed devils,
but after his first trip to mecca
he began to see the beauty of all peoples
how people of all backgrounds
came together in worship of the same deity

but less than a year after his new awakening
he was killed by his own people.

w.e.b. du bois

and i give reverence to
w.e.b. du bois

one of the most prolific philosophers of our time
who taught us it's better to free our minds
instead of playing the role
of the farmer
the sharecropper
the one who hips and hops
at the beck and call of whites...

this he argued with booker t.
who believed blacks should toil the lands
to prove equality

du bois said the souls of black folk
harbors the spirit of double consciousness

where blacks had to dance & smile
just to stay alive

and only on those lonely nights
were they truly allowed to thrive...

but who were they?

some played the role so well
it was too hard to tell

just who johnny ray and daisy mae were
when they exited the stage...

bobby seale and huey newton

and i give reverence to
bobby seale and huey newton

who taught blacks to defend themselves
when police were brutal

taught them to take up arms
and feed the community.

the panthers turned the courts upside down
had the police looking nervous when they came around...

threatened at the sight of powerful black men
who refused to bow down
in allegiance,
the government began to infiltrate
its core, withdrawing
federal aid
in hopes of bringing them to their knees.

somehow, they forgot to mention to include the violence
enacted against blacks that sparked the start
of the black panther party for <u>self-defense</u>

you see, that's the part they chose to miss...

aurelia, claudette, mary louise, and susie

and i give reverence to
aurelia, claudette, mary louise, and susie

those women who sat stern on montgomery buses before
rosa parks
whose acts of defiance sparked the bus boycott

mobilized the black masses for a common cause
and for that

--we must all pause...--

and remember the 382 days blacks walked all over
montgomery
breaking the back of the city economy

until the signs of segregation came tumbling down

382 days later, the walls came tumbling down!

rev. frank dukes

and i give reverence to
rev. frank dukes

who led miles college students
producing
a campaign of "selective buying"
of birmingham's department stores
when boycotting was legal no more

city leaders tried to underestimate the power
of the black dollar,
but they turned and cowered
once that $4 million dollars blacks spent --
became nonexistent.

you see, dukes was a different kind of man
he served his country in the war,
but returned home having to enter into back doors
and not having dressing rooms for blacks in department
stores
was something he could <u>not</u> take anymore.

carolyn maul

and i give reverence to
carolyn maul

who had just left those four girls
when she received that call,
where the speaker only said,

"3 minutes."

dumbfoundedly, she interrogates
the speaker

--no response—

seconds later the church on sixteenth street
was rocked
thunder rolled

the sound of flailing cries and
flying debris took control

at 10:22 am heaven called home
<u>four</u> souls...

after years of distress
and despair
carolyn maul mckinstry's testimony
helped convict those responsible
for that sunday morning bombing

and now, 40 years later,
the souls of those 4 girls can finally be at rest
("go to sleep little baby")

corporal roman ducksworth, jr.

and i give reverence to
corporal roman ducksworth, jr.

who after serving almost 10 years in the service
got a little nervous
when he received word of his sick new child

so, he rushed to his wife's side

before arrival
officer kelly killed him with one bullet

--to the heart--

under the guise of jr. being a freedom rider

his killer, a friend of the family,
sent daddy ducksworth a letter
saying,
"if i would've known he was your son,
this wouldn't have happened."

daddy ducksworth retorted,
"regardless of whose son it was,
this shouldn't have happened."

jr. was buried with full military honors
with a 16 gun salute
and an <u>integrated</u> honor guard.

bert williams

and i give reverence to
bert williams

star of the ziegfeld follies

who danced and sang
onstage in blackface
humped his shoulders
whited his gloves
with a minstrel grin on his face.

you see, williams played the role
that got him paid
kept his family fed
gave him worldwide notoriety

created the first dance that crossed over
crossed over the ocean & gave a performance
for the king,
which back at home, didn't mean a thing

but his comedic act crossed party lines
gave him room to define
himself & who he was

when the blackface came off…
when the black paint finally came off.

the rev. dr. martin luther king, jr.

and i give reverence to
the rev. dr. martin luther king, jr.

who advocated nonviolence
in the most violent society

he said,
if they hit you
turn the other cheek
if they spit on you
turn the other cheek

dr. king gained worldwide notoriety
by spearheading the movement
across the racist south

but when he died
a part of me died
that fearless connection was now lost

i felt like i, too, had paid the ultimate cost

we've come a long way, but where do we go from here?
we've made it through hell, i know Heaven must be near…

i've walked with kings and queens ii
(a part of me died)

june 12, 1963

the day medgar evers died
a part of me died

i wanted to register every negro in the whole world to vote!

sacrifice <u>my</u> life so the whole world could take note
that there shouldn't be any preferential racial treatment

we're one in the same, there's no use in trying to defeat me.

instead of us fighting civilly
in the land of the free
we should band together as
"…one nation under God
indivisibl[y]…"

medgar evers only wanted freedom for his people

equality for his people
was surely coming through his devoted work with the
n. double a c. p.

but
a piece of my spirit died
that night when his children anxiously anticipated his
arrival

eyes weary with sleep
but no sleep was to be found

they just <u>had</u> to see their daddy

but what they didn't see
was that sniper across the street

what they didn't see

was his name on the bullets that took life from him

what they didn't see
was the racial intensity permeated deep in mississippi

leaving his beautiful wife a weeping widow
alone in an empty bed

with an extra pillow…

september 15, 1963: girls

the day carol, denise, addie mae, & cynthia died
a part of me died

an increased feeling of revenge,
of despair
was birthed inside

their murders left a grieving ache in people's hearts
worldwide

left many re-thinking their racist mentalities and life
forcing them to come to grips with the immorality of
segregation,
discrimination,
which guided their ancestors for <u>many</u> generations

--not even in the church could little girls be safe--

killed because at the wrong time they were in the wrong
place
killed because the movement was moving at too fast of a
pace
killed because of the belief in the intrinsic inequality of those
of the black race

little girls
little girls
taken from this physical world
and placed up in grace

little girls
little girls
who will protect them from a world
steeped in hate?

little girls
little girls
who can no longer attain their own
aspirations

little girls
little girls
were now eternally freed from
racial exasperation.

like Jesus, their deaths turned over a new leaf,
waved a new tide

that old era of sheer legal segregation
had finally died.

neither black folk nor white folk could deny
the coming of the promised land
appearing before our anxious eyes...

september 15, 1963: boys

the day virgil lamar ware & johnny robinson died
was the same day the four little girls died,
but no one seems to remember their deaths;
or how their sacrifices allowed us to bask in freedom's
wealth;
or how it allowed us to exist in this <u>great</u> day our ancestors
could only <u>hope</u> for.

it was on their welted, bloody backs that we made it over
it was by <u>their</u> stripes that <u>we</u> were made healed
it was their tragedies that turned into our triumphs

their losses
gained <u>so</u> much for our people
allowed us to achieve <u>so</u> much as a people
instilled <u>so</u> much hope in our people
that we can't live our lives today
without giving reverence
to our people
who came before us
who sat at the table before us
and prepared a hearty meal <u>just</u> for us

i give reverence to
those who lived to fight the fight
i give reverence to
those who lost their plight in murder

--just like johnny and virgil--

and to you, virgil,
you may have been too young to comprehend
the rationalization of those white men
who foolishly took your life
as you rode innocently on the handlebars
of your brother's bike, but

rest assured that their dirty deed didn't go unpunished.

the law of the land may have freed them,
but when your blood called out from the ground,
the law of the Heavens called for vengeance.

and, to you, johnny,
your story is very pertinent
even almost 49 years later
because our men are still finding themselves as important
pieces of the policeman's puzzle.

when fully constructed
the black man is completely <u>de</u>constructed.

thus, removing the biggest threat the white man has ever
seen

your story teaches us that we still have a duty to fulfill:
"to protect and serve" our black men

october 31, 1963

the day my uncle herman died
a part of my mama died
took away her heart's very core
and she was never able to truly love anymore.

she could never get beyond his prophetic words
spoken just days before
saying to everyone
he was "tired" and was "going home."

and even in the forty nine years since
the mere mention of his name
<u>still</u> has a way of making the tears flow free.

she <u>still</u> hasn't been able to make peace.

my uncle herman, at age 6,
didn't know black boys were dispensable

he couldn't even begin to comprehend
the level of racism that dragged him 90 feet
down that clear birmingham street
that evening of 1963.

my mama, at age 5,
my other aunts & uncles as kids
had to watch their brother's killer go free

<u>no</u> police   <u>no</u> court case   <u>no</u> justice

--it was like nothing ever happened.--

what that white yellow cab driver & the racist system he
was bred in
took from my mama
was her ability to live rightfully in her own mind

mind jaded by the despair of dealing with a traumatic
situation
at too young of an age

--no therapy, no discussion--

because black folks knew an open mouth led to
fatal repercussions...

the effects of this situation has made its way to my
generation,
but i've learned to break that perpetual cycle
break it down into many, many pieces
and demand freedom for the whole of my people.

that halloween
was the date of death for my uncle,
my mama's childhood, and her sanity,
but those deaths
will not be the death of me

for his spirit lives within me

that's why i live for the freedom of my people

doing what i can to bring freedom to my people
saying what i can to be the voice of my people
speaking life to those dead of my people

and, today,

i refuse to have a part of me dead.

i live.

they hummed...

they hummed (oh, oh, mary!) they hummed (oh, oh, mary!)
they hummed (oh, oh, mary!) they hummed (oh, oh, mary!)

freedom songs grandma sang and sang
as her dishes and her pans clanked
and the water went down the drain, she
channeled the power of the God of abraham, she
summoned the strength of the women who paved her way,
she prayed
through quietly hummed prayer
she prayed

she remembered the lynchings of her uncles and her
brothers and
she remembered the light skin of her mothers and her
grandmothers, and
she remembered the hushing at her questioning, she
remembered her patience quickly lessening

she prayed
through quietly hummed prayer
she prayed

now, fannie lou hamer was a powerful woman
whose family survived off picking cotton
in m-i-s-s-i-s-s-i-p-p-i
(Lord, why?)

she knew this wasn't the life she should lead
that's why she joined that ol' sncc
affording blacks the guarantee of their names
on the voter registry
she was
jailed and beaten
with lasting damage to her eyes and kidney
battered and bleeding

oh, oh, mary!

but yet this soul sister didn't weep, she
spoke loudly at the democratic convention
giving her testimony full, sanctified conviction
describing experiences in a south so deep,
with a fervor so deep
it took almost a week
to comprehend the words that she speak
and she spoke

solidifying hope
that even in mississippi
black folk could have hope

they hummed (oh, oh, mary!) they hummed (oh, oh, mary!)
they hummed (oh, oh, mary!) they hummed (oh, oh, mary!)

now, shirley chisholm was the freedom sister
who refused to be bought or bossed, she
refused to be contained to a little, ol' box
she saw that glass ceiling and dared to go through it
fearlessly.

she set the standard in '72
for others to follow
when she dared to believe it was possible
for a woman black
to inhabit that house white
as commander-in-chief

instead of as the maid, or the little ol' nanny

and, yeah,
there were many who doubted her ability

there were many who doubted her prowess

but she stood firm in her hour

defying all traditional stereotypes

giving hope to others

non-male, non-white

that they, too, could rule the nation
from the desk of the oval office

they hummed (oh, oh, mary!) they hummed (oh, oh, mary!)
they hummed (oh, oh, mary!) they hummed (oh, oh, mary!)

the "s" on his chest

if i could pay homage to any man
i would pay homage to a real life superman
the one whose "s" on his chest
stands for "shuttlesworth"
and not some animated red & blue suited man.

i want to pay homage to a man who defied segregation
with a fully secured stance.

like that tree planted by the water.

and he… was not… moved.

i want to pay homage to a real life legend
one who stood tall when others fell short
one who looked bull connor
eye to eye, nose to nose
and never once backed down.

i want to pay homage to a real life legend
one who demanded freedom & nothing less
for his people.
one who walked out scotch free, burn free,
as the dynamite sticks sizzled underneath the cement.

you see when a man obeys God,
no man can touch him.

when a man is in God's hands,
not a man on earth can hurt him.

and because of his obedience to God's divine mission

--like noah in the Bible,
when he made it through the flood--

rev. shuttlesworth <u>literally</u> made it through the fi-yah!

so, if i can pay homage to a real life superman
i would pay it to the one whose "s" on his chest
stands for "shuttlesworth"
and not some animated red & blue suited man.

because it was <u>this</u> man
who instilled fear in the racist white south;

because it was <u>this</u> man
who was never known to hold his mouth—

or his tongue.

he was willing to do whatever it took to make freedom to
come.

and it came.

but not at a cost that was way too high
and not at a cost that he wasn't willing to pay--

and he paid.

by marching the streets with king and abernathy

he went to jail like a criminal that was serial
even putting his children on the front lines
of the movement when even
birmingham... adults... were... fearful...

many a cases came, and many a cases went,
but he was still willing to give of himself
in the name of his God and his people.

so, today, when i pay homage to this man
small in stature, but huge in grandeur,

i rock this "s" on my chest
as a visual representation of a <u>true</u> modern day legend.

i rock this "s" on my chest
as a reminder of his life and his works,
his charismatic attitude, and his courage.

i rock this "s" on my chest
for him boldly taking us where some preachers were too
afraid to go.

i rock this "s" on my chest
so, the younger generation will know of a <u>true</u> superman

one who exuded superhuman powers given divinely by God
to perform superhuman tasks to help everyday human
people
live equally in an unequal land
under the governmental guise of "liberty and justice for all"

and for all of this and much more, rev. shuttlesworth,
we are forever indebted & grateful.

i know the Lord has called your soul
and your flesh, from us, is now gone

so, in this hour,
we bid you to sleep well for
your work here on earth is done.

greens and jiffy cornbread

the urgency of the moment

this is a national alert!   this is a national alert!
this is a national alert!   this is a national alert!

please understand the urgency of the moment.

a great black man once said,
"she's got some good things to say
<u>even though</u> she's a woman!"

and i took the time to ponder
the audacity of an already oppressed man
to subjugate another

when this woman
had a womb and mammaries
just like his mother

shared the same pigment color

and even face to face
they mirrored each other.

please understand the urgency of the moment.

revolutionary freedom sister kathleen cleaver said,

"no one ever asks what a man's role was in the revolution."

so, i take the time to reinvent myself
just so you can hear my voice
in the outcry of lies and confusion

because now since everything is well
you want to try to overlook my endeavors as insignificant

--and <u>that</u> just doesn't make sense to me—
because i walked this cold, hard, earth with you
and was there to pick you up when you fell on your knees

i, along with sister
ida b. wells,
cried tears from bloodshot eyes
as they stared at the trees
that noosed the males in our families

i felt the same grief!

i felt the shame when they deprived me of my rights
and said i wasn't valuable enough to be considered equal

i had to fight

for everything i had
and i never thought it be against my own kind, but

for comments like,

"she got some good things to say
even though she's a woman!"

please understand the urgency of the moment.

racism!   sexism!
racism!   sexism!
racism!   sexism!

when will the day come
when there are no –isms?

for –isms are simply
schisms
created to divide and conquer peoples
physically,

literally,

it's incomprehensible to me
to demand freedom for yourself,
while denying freedom from others.

that's why is was
declared in 1776,

sentimentally refined in 1848,
considered again in 1863,
officially recognized in 1865,
systematically realized in 1920.
and for the rest of the century,
it was explored exponentially.

we began to truly understand the urgency of the moment.

hear our voices as they cry out in the silence:
the mothers
the teachers
the revolutionaries
the wives
the widows
the poets
the writers
the sisters

who made a difference.

these are their stories
and they will no longer go unheard.

please understand the urgency of the moment.

Written Collaboratively By:
LaQuita Middleton & Jessica Lockett

nappyminded ideology
http://www.Visionary-Tours.com

Author LaQuita Middleton-Holmes is available for
speaking engagements and poetic presentations.

For Booking Inquiries, Contact:

NEW GRIOT SOCIETY PRESS
PO BOX 91
BIRMINGHAM, AL 35201

(205) 467-8713

New Griot Society Press
ISBN-13: 978-0615724744
ISBN-10: 0615724744

Made in the USA
Lexington, KY
10 June 2015